TAMPA BAY RAYS
ALL-TIME GREATS

BY TED COLEMAN

Book design by Jake Slavik
Cover design by Jake Slavik

Photographs ©: David J. Phillip/AP Images, cover (top), 1 (top); Chris O'Meara/AP Images, cover (bottom), 1 (bottom), 4; John Cordes/Icon Sportswire, 6; VJ Lovero/SI/Icon Sportswire, 8; Cliff Welch/Icon Sportswire, 10, 18; Mitch Stringer/Icon Sportswire, 12; Larry Goren/Icon Sportswire, 14; Dan Hamilton/Icon Sportswire, 16; Sue Ogrocki/AP Images, 20

Press Box Books, an imprint of Press Room Editions.

ISBN
978-1-63494-511-0 (library bound)
978-1-63494-537-0 (paperback)
978-1-63494-587-5 (epub)
978-1-63494-563-9 (hosted ebook)

Library of Congress Control Number: 2022901756

Distributed by North Star Editions, Inc.
2297 Waters Drive
Mendota Heights, MN 55120
www.northstareditions.com

Printed in the United States of America
082022

ABOUT THE AUTHOR

Ted Coleman is a freelance sportswriter and children's book author who lives in Louisville, Kentucky, with his trusty Affenpinscher, Chloe.

TABLE OF CONTENTS

HERNÁNDEZ
39

CHAPTER 1
THE DEVIL RAYS

The Tampa Bay Rays played their first season in 1998. Back then, they were known as the Devil Rays. The team got some star power to start things off right. All-Star **Fred McGriff** had grown up in Tampa. So, when his hometown got a Major League Baseball (MLB) team, he signed there. McGriff was near the end of a great career. Still, he hit nearly 100 homers over five seasons with Tampa Bay.

Reliever **Roberto Hernández** had also already played many seasons in MLB. He proved to have plenty of pitching speed left.

HALL
44

Hernández recorded 43 saves in 1999. That remained a team record until 2010.

The Devil Rays didn't win many games in their early years. So, having Hernández protect leads was important. In the year that he saved 43 games, Tampa Bay won only 69 total.

Catcher **Toby Hall** provided key help to the pitching staff. The Devil Rays drafted him before the team had even played an MLB game. Hall went on to play the most games at catcher in team history.

Aubrey Huff stood out as one of the team's best power hitters. Huff slugged 128 home runs over seven seasons in Tampa. He played his strongest season with the Devil Rays in 2003. Huff hit .311 with 34 homers that year.

Defensive whiz **Julio Lugo** signed with Tampa Bay in 2003. The shortstop had excellent speed.

WADE BOGGS

Wade Boggs is best known for his Hall of Fame career with the Boston Red Sox. But he signed with his hometown Devil Rays in 1998. Boggs gave fans a memorable moment in 1999. He cranked out his 3,000th career hit that season. He became the first player to hit a home run for No. 3,000.

He stole 88 bases in his four seasons with the team. Lugo was also known for his power. He thrilled fans with long home runs.

When it came to speed, no Devil Ray could compete with **Carl Crawford**. Pitchers dreaded letting him reach base. Crawford became Tampa Bay's first true superstar. He swiped 50 or more bases in four different seasons. He also led the league in triples four times. Crawford's all-around skills made him a fan favorite. And he remained a key player when the team finally made a run to the postseason.

CAREER HITS
RAYS TEAM RECORD
Carl Crawford: 1,480

UPTON
2

CHAPTER 2
THE RAYS EMERGE

The 2008 season began a new era in Tampa. The team dropped the word "Devil" from its name and became known as the Rays. More importantly, the Rays reached the postseason for the first time. Center fielder **B. J. Upton** brought speed and great defense. He also became the first Ray to hit for the cycle.

Pitcher **Scott Kazmir** turned into the Rays' ace. The lefty threw blazing fastballs. And he had tons of raw talent. Kazmir debuted in 2004. By 2007, he led the American League (AL) in strikeouts.

PEÑA
23

James Shields joined Kazmir on the pitching staff in 2006. Shields threw many quality innings for Tampa Bay. But "Big Game James" was at his best when the Rays needed it most.

Ben Zobrist did a little of everything for the Rays. He played his first full season in 2009. That year, Zobrist played every position except pitcher and catcher. And he did it well. Zobrist made the All-Star team that season.

Most people didn't expect first baseman **Carlos Peña** to make the Rays in 2007. But he excelled in spring training and earned

JOE MADDON

Joe Maddon was hired as Tampa Bay's manager in 2006. The team had never made the postseason before. In the next nine seasons, Maddon led the Rays to the postseason four times. He won Manager of the Year twice. Maddon became known for developing the team's core of young players.

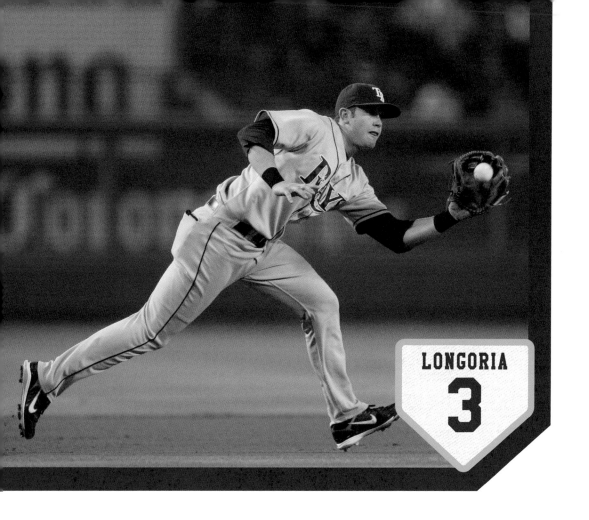

LONGORIA

3

a spot. He played the best year of his career that season, slugging 46 homers. That was a Rays record.

Third baseman **Evan Longoria** was Rookie of the Year in 2008. And that was just the start. He went on to have one of the best careers in team history. Longoria performed great on offense and defense. He made three All-Star teams and won three Gold Glove Awards. Longoria set many Rays records in his 10 seasons with the team.

During the 2008 postseason, rookie **David Price** pitched in a relief role. He even saved Game 7 of the AL Championship Series. That sent the Rays to their first World Series. Tampa Bay didn't win the Fall Classic. But getting there was a huge accomplishment for a team mostly known for losing. Price later set Rays records as a starting pitcher. In 2012, he became the first Rays player to win the Cy Young Award.

CHAPTER 3
THE RAYS KEEP SHINING

The Rays continued their success after the 2008 World Series run. They posted winning records in their next five seasons. They depended on Evan Longoria, David Price, and other key players. But they also kept adding more great young players.

Kevin Kiermaier wasn't known for his bat. But by 2015, he had established himself as one of the best center fielders in baseball. Kiermaier won his first of three Gold Glove Awards that year.

In the 2010s, the Rays became known for developing great pitchers. Starter **Alex Cobb**

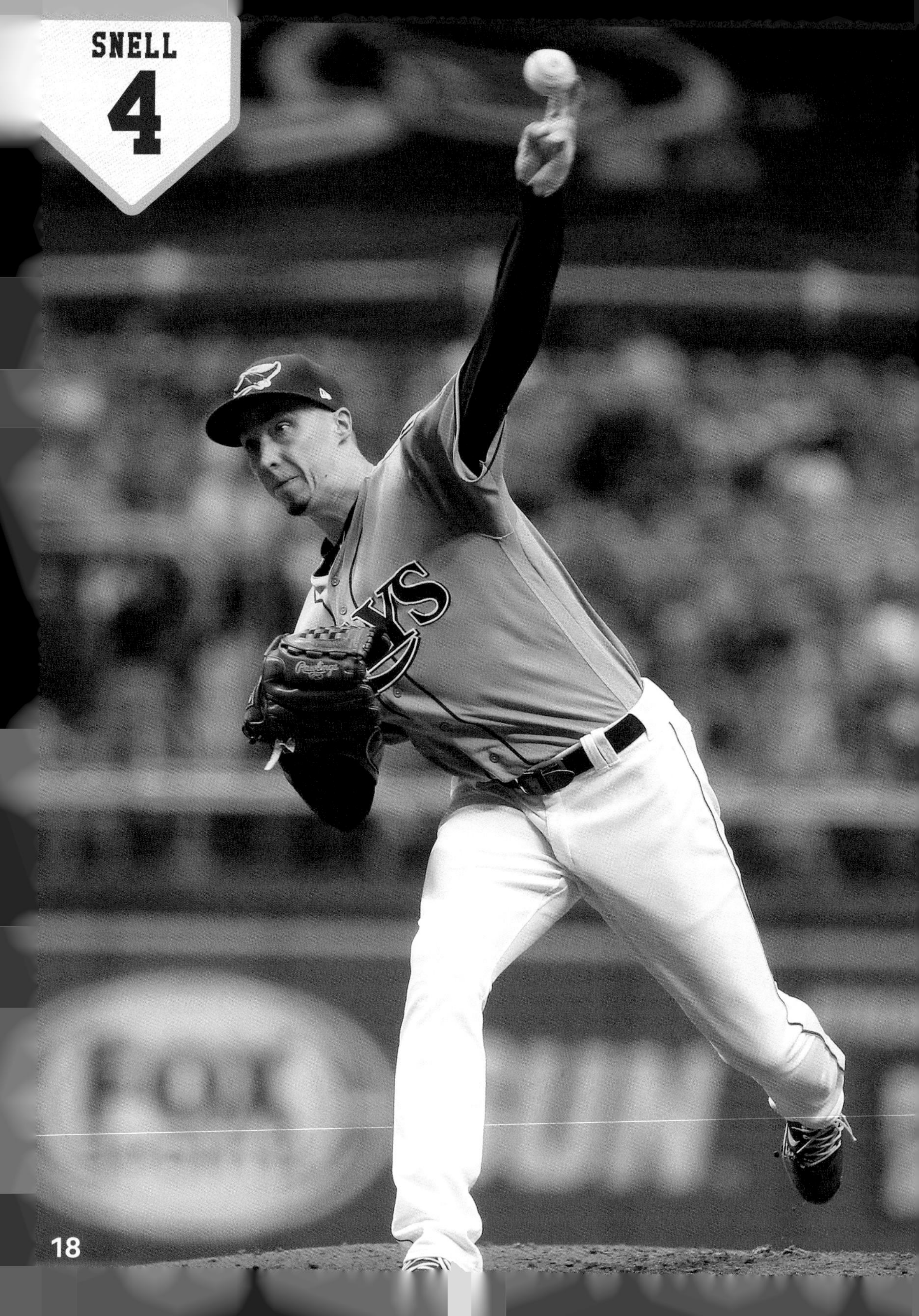
SNELL
4

posted an earned run average (ERA) of under 3.00 in both 2013 and 2014. However, an elbow injury stalled his career.

Blake Snell stepped up as the next great Rays pitcher. Snell struggled at first in the big leagues. But he broke out in 2018. That year, Snell won the Cy Young Award with a 21–5 record.

Snell's rotation mate **Chris Archer** was an All-Star in 2015 and 2017. Archer depended on a moving fastball and fast slider. He ranked right behind James Shields in career strikeouts.

The Rays returned to the postseason in 2019. Rookie **Brandon Lowe** made

STAT SPOTLIGHT

SINGLE-SEASON ERA
RAYS TEAM RECORD

Blake Snell: 1.89 (2018)

AROZARENA
56

the All-Star team that year. And in 2021, the slugging second baseman hit 39 homers.

The 2020 Rays made it back to the World Series. On the way, they discovered a franchise